STUMBLING STONES REMOVED FROM THE WORD OF GOD

By A. T. Pierson

Fountain of Life Ministries
MANHATTAN, ILLINOIS
www.hbcfrankfort.org

Stumbling Stones Removed From the Word of God
By A. T. Pierson
Cover Design by Joshua Jones

Published by Fountain of Life Ministries
202 Brynn Drive
Manhattan, IL 60442
www.hbcfrankfort.org

All rights reserved. No part of this publication may be reproduced, stored in a retrieval system or transmitted in any form by any means, electronic, mechanical, photocopy, recording or otherwise, without the prior permission of the publisher, except as provided by USA copyright law.

First Edition, 2012
Manufactured in the United States of America

Contents

A Word of Preface

We use the expression, "Stumbling Stones," merely by way of accommodation. The most devout and patient students of the Word of God fail to find inconsistencies, contradictions or real discrepancies in the Bible. All difficulties are due either to the imperfection of the medium of transmission, human language; or to the imperfection of the receptacle of the truth, the human mind itself. Our limited capacity, or our limited point of view and range of vision, may account for apparent imperfections, obscurities and disagreements in the Divine Word.

The purpose of this little book is not so much to reach those who accuse and assault the Inspired Word, as to help believers. That old Saint, Kleker, told D'Aubigne, that to remove one difficulty out of the way of a caviller only makes way for another; and that, if one will only take Christ as a complete Saviour and make a full surrender to Him, difficulties will commonly vanish. We believe that it is the heart that makes the theology; and that most of our doubts may be ultimately traced to an "evil heart of unbelief" that departs from the living God. Nevertheless even the most candid and reverent believer finds in the Word of God, especially in the English Bible, some difficulties or hindrances in the way of his understanding, if not of his faith; and such disciples it is our humble aim to help:

1. By removing unnecessary stumbling stones out of their way;
2. By enabling them to understand what may have been obscure;
3. By laying down certain laws or "canons" of Interpretation;

4. By exposing devices of Satan and other adversaries of the truth;
5. By showing the entire symmetry and self-consistency of the Truth itself.

Where real contradiction exists, Error must be present. Either the error lies in what we mistake for the truth, as a mirage is mistaken for a reality; or the error lies in our own organs of vision; our eye, being diseased, sees double where the object is single. A true believer runs no risk in calmly and resolutely examining into any alleged difficulty or discrepancy in the Bible. If one encounters a supposed ghost on a dark night, the best way is to walk up to it, and look it squarely in the face. To flee from a supposed apparition may leave a lingering doubt whether the ghostly illusion were a reality or not: a bold touch would have dispelled both the illusion and the doubt. To wait patiently and to search diligently is to find even the most formidable difficulties vanish, and to see the error to be one of our own ignorance or misapprehension. Nay, it often happens that stumbling stones become stepping stones, and hindrances are changed to helps.

Arthur T. Pierson.
2320 Spruce St, Philadelphia Pa.
October, 1890.

Contents

The Difficulties Stated

THE DIFFICULTIES STATED – THE CAUSES OF DISCREPANCIES.

The so-called 'discrepancies' of Holy Scripture may be classified as follows:

First, *verbal*, or such as concern the words or letters of Scripture;
Secondly, *historical*, or such as concern the names of persons and places, numbers, dates, and historical statements or events;
Thirdly, *moral*, or such as concern ethical precepts and principles, duties and relations; and,
Fourthly, *doctrinal*, or such as concern the direct doctrinal teaching of the word, especially as to the higher class of spiritual truths. The bibliography of this subject is quite extensive. Some fifty or more volumes have been published, which treat, more or less exclusively, this theme, one of which, by Mr. Haley, covers over five hundred pages. There are probably not less than five hundred other works which contain extended reference to these discrepancies; so that, in the effort to condense what needs to be written upon such a subject into a very brief compass, we find no little additional difficulty. But, as a bulky treatise would defeat our object, we shall simply group all the "discrepancies" together, and offer general suggestions and principles, covering various particulars in each class.

We begin, very naturally, by inquiring *whence these apparent discrepancies come*. What is their *source*?

The first general class are those which come from *variations in the mere letter* of Scripture.

I. *Errors in Transcription.*

In the absence of the printing press all copies of the Word of God were of course the product of the manual labor of scribes. Prof. Norton estimates that, by the end of the second century, there were sixty thousand manuscripts of the Gospel in existence; and, including manuscripts of the Old Testament, millions of copies of God's Word have doubtless been made in the course of the ages. From seven hundred to one thousand Greek manuscripts are now extant, of which fifty are one thousand years old, and some few are one thousand five hundred years old, whereas the oldest existing classic manuscript is not nine hundred. Of course the original manuscripts of the Bible have all disappeared, and God meant that they should, to save us from a similar idolatry to that which lifted the Brazen Serpent and Gideon's Ephod to divine honors.

In producing exact copies, perfect accuracy would be impossible without a perpetual miracle of divine supervision, as great as that of original Inspiration. Even in printed books it is found impracticable to secure entire freedom from errors; even when large rewards have been offered for their detection, new ones have been found after the two hundredth reading. How much more difficult to secure absolute accuracy when the first form is also the final form and there is no chance to correct "proof!"

In manual transcriptions mistakes are therefore inevitable.

1. *Hebrew letters often closely resemble each other.*

There are at least eight pairs of letters, so nearly alike as to be constantly mistaken for each other, like the English b and d, c and e, f and old-fashioned s, (ſ) 1 and t. Old manuscripts became faded and blurred, and this increased the liability of such errors, and mistakes in names and figures easily arose in this way, where the context and general sense furnished no guide.

2. It is probable that, both in the Hebrew and Greek manuscripts, *letters were anciently used for numerals.*

Warrington thinks that the letters of the alphabet, taken in their order, represented numerical values, as follows, units, tens and hundreds up to 400; 1, 2, 3, 4, 5, 6, 7, 8, 9, 10, 20, 30, 40, 50, 60, 70, 80, 90, 100, 200, 300, 400; that the *five terminal letters* supplied the numbers representing the even hundreds, from 500 to 900 inclusive; and that the thousands were represented by affixing marks or points to those representing units, etc.

Two sorts of mistakes might easily creep in; one letter might be mistaken for another of different value; or discrepancies might be introduced where the attempt was made to substitute the full word for the letter. There is scarcely a case in which copyists are believed to have made any intentional change in the original text. In one case, where the name Manasseh appears instead of Moses, some have thought that some officious scribe made the substitution to save the disgrace, to the great Jewish Lawgiver, of recording the idolatry of his grandson (Judges xviii. 30).

II. Errors in Punctuation.

In the original manuscripts there were probably no punctuation marks. In fact some manuscripts were *cursive*, i. e. the words were run together with no space between them. The translators have introduced punctuation marks, to make the sense obvious; and, for convenience, division into chapters and verses. Of course all this belongs to the human, uninspired, and therefore fallible element in the Modern Bible, and no objections, drawn from punctuation marks, or these arbitrary divisions, really lie against the Inspired Word of God, itself.

There are not a few instances in which this punctuation may have introduced at least a very doubtful sense or construction. A few examples may be given.

John xii. 27. “What shall I say? Father, save me from this hour: but for this cause came I unto this hour.” By substituting an *interrogation point* for the colon, after the word ‘hour,’ the sense is made much more clear.

Luke xiii. 24, 25. Omitting the period after the word ‘able,' or substituting a comma, we are taught that the risk lies in *seeking to enter when it is too late.* Compare Matthew xxv. 1-10.

Psalm cix. 6 to 19 inclusive. If these verses are *put in quotation marks,* as the ‘words of hatred,’ which, ‘with a lying tongue,’ the ‘adversaries’ of David ‘speak against him,’ this Psalm is made no longer his imprecation of curses on their heads, but his appeal to God in reply to their maledictions. Then the sudden change from the plural to the singular number, in verse 6 and following, is explained, and both the introductory and closing verses acquire a new and beautiful significance. Compare especially verses 28 to 31 with 1-3.

Examples of at least *doubtful division,* where the sense is very seriously interrupted or obscured, might be multiplied. A few will suffice.

1 Corinthians xii. 31. There should here be no division of chapters. The “more excellent way,” which Paul shows, is the *cultivation of Love*; and a colon after the word ‘way’

should be the only interruption to the sense. To introduce a new chapter breaks all continuity.

The connection between Chapters II. And III. of the Epistle to the Ephesians is similarly intimate; and the argument is perfect only as the break is avoided. “'For this cause” refers back to the truth set forth in the previous Chapter. Compare also Hebrews iii. 14. The word ‘therefore,’ at the beginning of the fourth Chapter, *depends upon* the sentiment immediately preceding. So xi., xii.

III. *Errors in Amplification.*

As translators have supplied punctuation points, so they have supplied *words and phrases*, to complete the sense or make the meaning obvious. As is well known, these supplied words are always indicated by the use of *italics*. The ignorant reader sometimes supposes that italicized words represent the *emphatic* words, and is perhaps betrayed into the error of the simple minded ‘Dunkerd’ preacher, who gravely read 1 Kings xiii. 27, thus: “And he spake unto his sons, saying, Saddle me the ass. And they saddled *him*!”

As to these italicized words, it has been seriously questioned whether they are, in any case, needful, helpful or *justifiable*. Where the original demands or implies them, they need not be italicized, since they are not really 'supplied' words; where the original does not so justify them, to introduce them may sometimes be to *introduce notions foreign to the meaning* of the Word and the mind of the Spirit; and may therefore be unwarrantable tampering with the Inspired Word of God. At the very least, we must remember that all italicized words belong, like punctuation points and chapter-and-verse divisions, to the fallible element, and therefore can never become the basis of objection to anything but the work of *translators*.

We append a few examples of supplied words. By reading the passages and *omitting* these italicized phrases, another meaning will often at once appear, and also a much clearer sense. In the examples given we omit the supplied words.

Matthew xx. 23. “But to sit on my right hand and on my left is not mine to give, but for whom it is prepared of my Father.” So read, Christ does not limit his own power to give the chief places, save that it must be exercised in union with the Father.

John iii. 34. “For God giveth not the Spirit by measure”—doling out the supply as if his resources were limited.

John viii. 6. “But Jesus stooped down, and with his finger wrote on the ground.” In Syria and the East, to this day, writing with the finger in the sand is a common method of teaching, as with us the slate and blackboard are used. It introduces a possibly unwarranted conception, to add, “*as though he heard them not.*”

James i. 25. “Whoso looketh into the perfect law of liberty and continueth.” The figure is that of a mirror, and the word ‘continueth’ may refer to the *looking*. We must not simply *glance* but gaze at ourselves as seen in that law, continue looking so that the impression may be permanent.

Psalm xxii. 1, 3, 11 etc. Bishop Alexander calls this prophetic poem of the Crucified, a ‘PSALM OF SOBS.’ It represents the vicarious sufferer as in dying agonies, able only to articulate a few words at a time: and the fragmentary character of the utterances is one of the most remarkable features of the plaint. To supply words, and so make every sentence complete, interferes with the impression which the Spirit would convey. How much more pathetically majestic if translated literally!

"My God! My God!
Why hast Thou forsaken me!
Far from helping me! –
Words of my roaring!" –
etc.

We have no space for multiplying examples; but refer the reader to a few additional cases where the omission of the supplied words will suggest a new and often higher sense.

Deut. xxxii. 35.
Psalm x. 4; xiv. 1; l. 8; li. 12.
Proverbs xxvii. 19.
Isaiah xxvi. 19.
Malachi iii. 10. "'Until failure of enough," i. e. *until the supply fails!*
Mark xvi. 20.
John xx. 11.
Hebrews xi. 21.
2 Peter iii. 17.

IV. *Difficulties Incident to Translation.*

In all human language necessary imperfection inheres; and yet the Holy Spirit was compelled either to invent a new nomenclature which would have been unintelligible to man, or else to use that imperfect medium with which he is familiar. So far as language is merely the mould of thought, or thought is the mould of language, the two must correspond: and we shall find things, divine and spiritual, inadequately conveyed by human words, and in some cases absolutely no word will be found fit to be the vehicle or mould of a divine conception.

From this general source proceed a great variety of infelicities, inaccuracies, and even apparent contradictions, that are purely linguistic and verbal.

1. Material terms are necessarily employed to express immaterial things: the spiritual is cramped and confined by the carnal wrappings.

The word 'spirit' from *spiro*, I breathe, means, in its Hebrew and Greek equivalents, literally wind or breath. To infer that the spirit of man or of God is simply breath, would be to limit a divine conception by the narrow literalism of the best word that human language can furnish to convey the thought.

When Jewish writers speak of the "*tongue* of events," meaning thereby God's acts translated into the language of historical occurrences, no one misunderstands the phrase.

2. *Figurative* terms are also necessarily employed, but must not be literally construed. The Oriental habit of mind is peculiarly luxuriant and imaginative. Eastern idioms abound in bold and striking metaphors and even hyperbole. "To construct dogmas out of such materials, would be like attempting to build a palace out of sunbeams and rainbows." As Prof. Park says, there is manifestly a wide gap between oriental minstrelsy and occidental logic.

3. Much language, applied to God, is really applicable only to man, is *Anthropomorphic*, and *Anthropopathic*, i. e., drawn from the human form and passions.

When we read of the '*Fingers* of God,' with which He wrote on the Tables of Stone; the '*Feet* of God,' which rest on the earth as His footstool; the '*Eyes'* and '*Eyelids* of God,' which 'behold' and 'try' the children of men; of the '*Nostrils* of God,' into which the sweet incense of worship ascends, etc., these terms are Anthropomorphic and must be so understood.

Isa. iii. 13. The Lord standeth up to plead.
Joel iii. 12. There will I sit to judge all the heathen.

It would seem incredible that any one, even a caviller, could call such statements ‘discrepancies.’ This is an example of the uncandor and unfairness of much so-called ‘criticism.’ Such language is simply drawn from the habits of Oriental courts, where advocates *stand up to plead,* and judges *sit down* to pronounce sentence. God is likewise said to “Come down," when He interposes in human affairs, which belong to a subordinate sphere: and such terms as “ascend” and “descend” are often used with reference to the comparative elevation of the subjects and objects to which the attention is turned.

Most words are *tropes*, concealing a figure. Contradictions frequently disappear, as soon as we cease to insist on an absurd literalism.

Invisible things may be clearly seen; (Rom. i. 20) and we may *look at* what is unseen. (2 Cor. iv. 18.)

4. Metaphors are often *mixed*, because one figure does not suffice to express the full meaning.

Ps. xviii. 1,2. David calls the Lord, his “strength, rock, fortress, deliverer, buckler, horn and high tower.” Here are at least seven different metaphors. The inconsistency is rhetorical but not real: in fact there is sublimity in the very mixture. Peter says “stablish, strengthen, settle you,” and Paul says, “rooted and grounded in love.” One expression being inadequate, the writer leaps at once to another, that the combination may convey what neither would alone.

5. *Language of Appearance* is close akin to figurative terms, and is always allowable.

When the sun is represented as ‘rising’ or ‘setting;’ or the dew as ‘distilling’ and ‘descending from heaven,’ we are not warranted either in construing these terms literally, or in objecting to them because of scientific inaccuracy. In this scientific age we use such terms while conceding their inexactness, because they describe appearances and belong to the popular idiom.

6. *Various renderings of the same original word,* lead to inevitable confusion.

John xv. 4, 9, 11, one Greek word (μενω) is variously translated, abide, remain, continue, etc.

1 Cor. ii. 15, the same Greek word ανακρινεται is translated discern, and judge.

7. Words are sometimes invested by the reader with a *wrong sense.*

"God is angry with the wicked." Ps. vii. 11.
He is the "*Avenger*" of evil, 1 Thess. iv. 6.
Wrath is ascribed even to the "Lamb." Rev. vi. 16.

These and similar terms are to be used and understood in a higher sense than the ordinary one. Anger is not, in itself, a sin: in fact, without holy indignation, there is no perfectly holy character. The verbs, '*avenge*' and '*revenge*' and the corresponding nouns, '*vengeance*' and '*revenge*' mean different things: the former verb and noun refer to a public governmental, judicial act, which is necessary to the upholding of law; [Jer. li. 56] while 'revenge' refers generally to a *private, personal act* of retaliation. There is a manifest and broad distinction between a ruler calmly requiting or recompensing evil, for public good, and an injured party passionately returning evil for evil, for private gratification. God is never vindictive but always vindicative, i. e. He vindicates law. "*Odit errores, amat errantes*." When *wrath* is ascribed to Him, we are to remember it is *holy* wrath and so a part of His infinite perfections. A magnetic needle has polarity, and by the same law it *attracts* and *repels* at the same pole. Benevolence is an attribute whose two poles are,

Love and Wrath. *By the same principle*, God both loves holiness and hates sin; and, because He is capable of holy complacence toward the good, must be capable of holy repulsion toward evil.

The word, '*hate'* is often used of a *lesser love*. Compare Rom. ix. 13. Luke xiv. 26.

"God *hardened* Pharaoh's heart." Exod. ix. 12. This implies in God no complicity with evil. He withdrew softening influences which were abused. Nay more: the same sun melts the wax, and bakes and cakes the clay; and so the same influences which soften and subdue the obedient, harden the rebellious. Pharaoh's wilfulness naturally produced the same effect as did God's judicial infliction. Compare Exod. viii. 15, 32.

In the narrative about David and the Ammonites, etc., in 2 Sam. xii. 31, it is said he "*put them under* saws, harrows, axes," and "made them *pass through* the brick-kiln." Sceptics unwarrantably construe this *subjection of the people to certain forms of labor*, as though it were meant that David cut them in pieces or burned them alive. In 1 Chron. xx. 3, the word "*cut*,"' is probably a mistake. A Hebrew word, as much like the other as 'cut' is like 'put,' and even more like it, is accidentally mistaken for it. (*Vayyasar for vayyasem.*)

Paul says, "concerning virgins I have no *commandment of the Lord*."' 1 Cor. vii. 25. Are we to understand him as disclaiming inspired guidance in the case? or does he simply mean that whereas, in counsels *to the married*, he has referred them to an express recorded commandment of the Lord, Mal. ii. 14-16, Matt. xix. 6, 9; in this case there is *no such written commandment* to which to appeal? Compare 1 Cor. vii. 6, 10. When he says, "I think also that I have the Spirit of God," 1 Cor. vii. 40, it might be rendered, I think that I also have the Spirit (καγω), i. e. as well as others who claim to be your teachers, and are not inspired apostles.[1] So understood, instead of disclaiming inspiration, he rather affirms with peculiar emphasis the apostolic warrant for his instruction.

The Israelites borrowed of the Egyptians, Exod. xii. 35. "Borrowed" probably means 'demanded,' as the price of departure.

"The bears *tare* forty and two of them," 2 Kings ii. 24. It is not said that they *killed* any of them.

Abraham was commanded to "*offer*" Isaac for a burnt offering. Gen. xxii. 2.

It is not said, anywhere, that God commanded him to *slay* his son, though the father so interpreted it. God intended that he should *present Isaac as an offering*, and that is what he did. It is probably part of the inspired perfection of the Scriptures that words are used with such discrimination; and it is therefore the duty of every reader to note *exactly what is said,* lest he carelessly introduce a conception, foreign to the real narrative.

V. *Errors of Interpretation.*

Where no fault can reasonably be found with either the original or the translation, the *reader's misapprehension* may cause difficulty. We must therefore learn to interpret the language of the Bible intelligently and correctly. Several facts are to be borne in mind.

1. Words often *change meaning*, and are liable to be misunderstood.

'Prevent' means to go before, or anticipate. 1 Thess. iv. 15.

---

[1] J. H. Brookes, D.D.

'Let' means not to *let*, i. e. to hinder.2 Thess. ii. 7.
'Conversation' means course of life. Heb. xiii. 5.

2. The *same word* is used in *different senses*.

Compare Exod. xxxi. 17, with Isa. xl. 28. Though God "fainteth not neither is weary," yet "He rested and was refreshed." 'Rest' sometimes means repose after fatiguing labor, or, as in this case, *cessation from activity*, the arresting of work.

Adam was said to '*hide*,' and Jonah to '*flee*,' from 'the Presence of the Lord.' Yet we are taught that to flee or to hide from His presence is impossible. Ps. cxxxix. 7. There is an *omni-presence* of God which equally pervades all space; but there is a *manifested* Presence, such as, in the Garden of Eden or in the Sanctuary of old, was often visible and audible. We are told that God "was not in the wind," the "earthquake" or the "fire;" but the meaning is that He was not specially and personally manifested in these forms, as He was in the "still small voice" which followed them. 1 Kings xix. 11, 12.

The word "*covet*" is used in Exod. xx. 17, of unlawful desire after that which is another's; in 1 Cor. xii. 31, of a holy yearning to possess that which will benefit another.

"Christ was made sin for us," though He "knew no sin," 2 Cor. v. 21, i.e. He was made a sin-offering, accounted judicially as a sinner.

"*Tempt*" may mean to put to proof, to test: or to entice to sin. Compare Gen. xxii. 1, Deut. vi. 16, and Jas. i. 13.

"*Cleave*" may mean, to cling to, or to part from, another. Rom. xii. 9. Zech. xiv. 4.

“Devoted” means consecrated to holy uses, or, sometimes, doomed, to destruction.

The verb “*have*” is used in Matt. xiii. 12, both of nominal and of real possession. Mr. Haley cites a couplet from Dryden's *Juvenal*, in illustration of a like usage:

> “Tis true poor Codrus nothing had, to boast;
> And yet poor Codrus all that nothing lost.”

To “*seek early*” may also mean to seek earnestly. Compare Prov. i. 28, viii. 17. In one case the earnestness of the pious youth, and in the other of the despairing and hardened sinner, is referred to: a holy longing after God's favor is contrasted with a desperate effort to evade sin's penalty and God's judgment.

The word “*evil*” may mean perverse, iniquitous, or merely adverse, calamitous.

"*Jealousy*" sometimes represents "the rage of man" a mean, malicious suspicion; and, again, a holy affection which by its nature admits no rivalry. God is said to be “*jealous*” because He can allow no other object to share His people's devotion, without sanctioning idolatry.

The phrase “*the righteousness of saints*” sometimes seems to refer to *justification*; at other times to *sanctification*; and at others to *resurrection life*. It is of great importance that we learn to discriminate between these three. Justification is a divine *act*, *imputing* to us a righteousness *complete but not inherent*. Sanctification is a divine *work*, *imparting* to us a righteousness *inherent but not complete*. Resurrection life implies a finished work, when our righteousness is *both* inherent and complete.

3. Words are used both in an *absolute*, and in a *relative* sense.

God who “changes not,” is said to "repent."

There is no contradiction. It is because He absolutely changes not, that He relatively changes. If a movable body revolves about a fixed object, their relative positions are constantly changing: if both were moving, their relative positions might remain the same. When a man who has been turned *from* God turns toward Him, God is *in effect* turned also toward the man, though in fact there has been in God Himself no change. The attitude of the sinner relatively affects the attitude of God. We say, “the sun shines” or “does not shine," when in fact it always shines; but the position of the earth, or the interposition of the clouds, intercepts its rays.

Christ says “my Father is greater than I;” yet He also affirms “I and my Father are one;” and Paul claims for Him such equality with God as that the claim implies no robbery of God. Compare Jno. xiv. 28, Phil. ii. 5, 6. In one case, Christ speaks of His relative position as a *Son*, or as *Messiah*, the Sent one: in the other His absolute, essential equality is referred to, as one member of a firm, where all members are equal in the property invested and the rights implied, might still disclaim all authority in a certain department of the business, which by mutual agreement is committed to another partner.

4. Words are used sometimes of the *intent* and again of the *effect*, of an act or course.

“In so doing thou shalt heap coals of fire on his head.” Rom. xii. 20. Here not the *design*, but the *result*, of kindness to an enemy is indicated. The silversmith does not perfectly melt the metal until, in addition to the fire beneath the crucible, he heaps the hot coals on the top of the silver. When we heap kindness on an enemy's head, we have him between two fires: the conscience of the man accuses him, and our tenderness combines with that to melt him.

“I came not to send peace but a sword.” Matt. x. 34, 36; i. e. though Christ's desire and design are to give peace, the effect of his coming is to make division and separation between those who serve God and those who serve Him not. We must discriminate between the *object* and the *effect* of His mission.

When it is said that, at Nazareth, “He *could do* no mighty work" (Mark vi. 5), it is no contradiction of the fact that “All Power” is his. Matt. xxviii. 18. He chooses to be limited, in His beneficent activity, by human unbelief. He could do mighty works among those Nazarenes, only by disregarding the bounds which He had wisely adopted for moral ends.

Under this same subdivision we may *include* promises which are in some cases absolute, and in others *conditional.*

VI. *Freedom in the Use of Names.*

1. Multiplicity of names for the same person

Peter is also called Simon, Cephas, Simon Bar-Jona, Simeon, Simon Peter, Simon son of Jonas. Joseph is also called Barsabas and Justus. Jacob is also Israel. Edom is Esau, Gideon is Jerubbaal. Saul is Paul.

2. Names of *persons* are changed; and names of persons and *places* are often interchanged. e.g., Edom.

In the deficiency of other methods of recording and transmitting history, individual men and women became themselves marks, memorials or monuments of crises or turning points, or new departures.

Thus Abram's name was changed to Abraham, and Sarai's to Sarah. Gen. xvii. 5, 15.

Jacob's name was changed for a similar reason to Israel. Gen. xxxii. 28.

Neander's name before conversion was David Mendel. The change marks his regeneration — the 'new-man.'

VII. In *writing numbers*, oriental usage was often singular.

1. In the expression of aggregates.

Nordheimer says: Hebrew and Arabic allow peculiar latitude in the use and expression of numbers. Both languages allow one to write units, tens, hundreds, thousands, in succession or in reverse order. Much obscurity at times occurs, as if one should write, "five and twenty and two hundred and ten thousand." This might be understood to mean an aggregate number as small as 10, 225, or as large as 210, 025.

2. Round numbers were used for convenience, or in symbolism. e.g., a week, called eight days. Jno. xx. 26.

VIII. *Difference of dates* is sometimes the source of apparent discrepancy or discordance.

The disagreeing statements refer to different periods. What was once true ceases to be at a subsequent time.

Compare Gen. i. 31, and Rom. viii. 22. When God first made all things, he pronounced everything "very good." After sin's blight and curse came upon it, the whole creation groaned and travailed in pain together.

IX. Different modes of reckoning.

1. The civil and sacred years of the Hebrews differed.

Abib, the first month of the *sacred* year, was the seventh month of the *civil* year. Compare the “old style” and the “'new style,” eleven days apart.

2. *Fractional* days and years were reckoned as whole ones. With the Rabbins, the very first day of a year sometimes stood for the whole year. — Lightfoot. Parts of a day were reckoned for the whole: e.g. , Christ's “three days” in the grave, though He appears to have been in the sepulchre a part of the sixth, the whole of the seventh and a part of the eighth.

X. History in Bible usage is often made *subordinate to prophecy and symbolism.* In other words the historical accuracy is of less account than the prophetical or symbolical or ethical teaching which the history expresses and embodies.

E.g., Israel's history, as a nation, is not counted on the strict historical scale, but on the prophetic. When God's ancient people relapsed into idolatry and virtual apostasy, and were given over into captivity, their normal and *prophetic history* stopped: they were *not reckoned as having any history.* Only when such a principle is understood and applied to the record, can we make out the biblical computations of time, as applied to this elect nation.

We notice various cycles of 490 years, or ten Jubilees, which seem to constitute a sort of unit of measurement in the Old Testament. The 480 years of 1 Kings vi. 1, between Israel's going forth and Solomon's temple building, do not count, as a recent writer has observed, the seven periods of servitude. The actual time is 611 years. Deducting for servitude 131 years, we have 480. Then add, for building and furnishing the temple, 10 years, and we have 490.

From that period to the return from Babylon, in the time of Nehemiah, is 560 years. Deduct for captivity, 70 years, and we have again 490.

So the 490 years in the seventy Heptades of Dan. ix. cannot be made out accurately, unless we omit the periods of interrupted fellowship with God and disobedience to His will. In fact the crucifixion of Christ appears to have interrupted the last "week," and at least half of it seems to be the prophetical "three and a half years," "'forty and two months," or 1260 days of the Apocalypse.

> XI. *One event or truth or subject* has *different sides and aspects*. We must get the point of view, and even the plane of thought, occupied by the sacred writer or speaker.

1. Truth is many-sided.

Every truth or fact has at least two faces. To look at it from one direction or side, only, gives us only a half truth, which, if we consider it the whole, is a half error. Apposite truths are not opposites. There is no antagonism between them, but rather complementism: they are the hemispheres which together complete the sphere.

Hence truths that at first appear to conflict may have often the highest harmony and be necessary to each other.

Man is at the same time mortal and immortal. He may be buried, and yet it is equally true that he cannot be: or, as Socrates said, "You may *bury me* if you can *catch me*."

2. Character has complex relations.

Christ is at once a lion and a lamb, Rev. v. 5, 6; a priest and victim, Heb. viii. 1, ix. 26-28; a shepherd and sheep, Jno. x. 11, Acts. viii. 32; the door to the fold and the pastor to the flock, Jno. x. 7. 11.

3. Different experiences and conditions may pertain to the same person, at the same time.

Christ's peace was the perfect peace of God, even while he sweat as it were great drops of blood.

Dr. Payson in dying was both in intensest agony and intensest ecstasy.

4. The same *subject* may be treated from different points of approach and survey, for different ends.

Thus Matthew, Mark, Luke and John, each writing for a different class of readers, — Jews Romans, Greeks, and believers in general, will each emphasize a different aspect of the complex character of Jesus.

Matthew lays stress on Him as Messiah — King of the Jews. Mark lays stress on Him as mighty God, miracle worker. Luke lays stress on Him as the Son of man. John lays stress on Him as the Son of God. Compare the books of Kings and Chronicles; one being the annals of the Kingdom, the other the history of the Hierarchy.

For similar reasons, some authors may follow the *chronological,* while others follow the *logical*, order; others, without regard to historical connection or sequence, may group *ethical* teachings together.

5. Consequently, to avoid partial and incomplete views, we must *compare scripture with scripture* until each half truth finds its complementary half.

The parable of the "Pounds" and of the "Talents" must be taken together. Thus combined they present the whole law of *God's administration of gifts*. Where gifts are equal, but unequally improved, the rewards are unequal: where gifts are unequal, but equally improved, the rewards are equal. Compare Luke xix., Matt. xxv.

In Luke xv., we have not three parables, but *one* parable with three forms of presentation. The first and second emphasize *God's* part in recovering the lost sinner; the third brings to the front *man's* part both in wandering and return.

Paul emphasizes *faith*: James, *works*. There is no conflict. Paul was rebuking Pharisaic dependence on self-righteous works. James was contending against antinomian dependence on a mere creed. James probably uses the word "justify" in the sense of manifesting or proving. Thus faith justifies the soul, works justify the faith.

XII. *Condensation of narratives* accounts for some incongruities.

1. For the sake of brevity, or because a specific purpose, which is controlling, demands only the salient points of a narrative, a few characteristic features are presented and the account is fragmentary. Were all the missing links furnished, no real difficulty would remain.

2. The imagination or hasty inference of critics may often supply an incongruous link where God has left an unfilled vacancy.

Some professedly religious teachers have shocked the sensibilities of all true and reverent believers by using such phrases as the""errors," "mistakes" and even "immoralities" of scripture.

For example, Exod. xxi. 24, "An eye for an eye," etc., is adduced as a scriptural sanction, justifying private revenge and retaliation of injuries. But who is authorized to say that this authorizes the exaction of private and personal vengeance? May it not be the law by which the judges were guided in the *judicial infliction of penalty?* The brief narrative leaves many gaps to be supplied. In Patriarchal times, with imperfect legislation and government, such penalties may have been the most salutary preventives of acts of violence, and especially of maiming.

> XIII. *Different events or persons may be confused* on account of *similar features.*

On a larger or smaller scale, history is constantly repeating itself. Abram twice equivocated concerning Sarah; Isaac imitated his father's example, in the case of Rebekah. David twice and in very similar circumstances spared Saul's life, etc.

There were, in modern times, two Jonathan Edwards, father and son. Both were grandsons of clergymen and, themselves, clergymen. Both were pious and precocious youths, famous scholars, and tutors for equal periods in their respective colleges. Both succeeded, in their respective charges, their maternal grandfathers, were dismissed on account of peculiar religious opinions; were again settled over congregations singularly attached to them, and employed leisure hours in favorite studies, and in preparation, for publication, of works of value. Both left their parishes for college presidencies, and died shortly after inauguration, with but one year's difference in their respective ages, one being fifty-six, the other fifty-seven; and both, on the first sabbath of the fatal year, preached from the same text, "This year thou shalt surely die." (Haley, 27).

Modern critics who seek to prove that similar biblical narratives are a confusion of historical facts, and refer to the same person or event, can in no case adduce by comparison of scriptural accounts any parallel to the coincident features of these two remarkably similar lives and careers. And were the methods of the "Higher Criticism" adopted in this case, some may yet arise who will seek to prove that there was after all but *one* Jonathan Edwards!

XIV. Special laws or principles apply to the *Interpretation of Prophecy.*

Prophecy is the *language of the future.* It is a well known fact that as we look ahead, in a direct linc, ccrtain optical illusions are the result:

First, *Perspective*: objects at different distances are seen in one limited field of vision and lying within the same narrow arc.

Secondly, *Foreshortening*: objects, far separated from us and from each other, appear near and closely related; what is stretched out over vast length, is seen shortened — hence the term "foreshortening," to express the apparent shortening from the fore-view. Only by experience does the mind learn to detect and correct the errors of the eye. Similar illusions pertain to the careless reading of prophecy.

1. In prophecy we often see two or more events of a similar character outlined by a common profile. One outline properly portrays two events, one on a smaller, and the other on a larger scale; one nearer, the other more remote.

E.g., Matt. xxiv. where the destruction of Jerusalem is the type of the End of the Age, and prophecies concerning both are closely intertwined because one general profile answers for both.

2. Events may appear in a common field of vision, all of which are future, which and, as they occur, will be seen to be

marked by many distinct and distinguishing features.

3. Future events, far separated in point of time, may be so mingled on the horizon of prophecy, as to appear, like mountains in a range, near to each other.

4. *History* may be communicated *prophetically*, i.e. by a backward instead of a forward vision.

Hugh Miller believed that the six days of creation were revealed to Moses after some such manner, as a series of spectacular or dramatic scenes, to be interpreted after the manner of prophecy.

XV. There is a *Progress in Revelation*, from Genesis to the Apocalypse.

1. Things, veiled at first, even when revealed in form, were afterward fully unveiled as revelation became clearer. This is the force of the word, “mystery,” in the New Testament.

And here we may possibly find the key to many so-called discrepancies.

E.g., quotations from the Old Testament Hebrew or the Septuagint, or Greek Alexandrian version, are found in the New Testament in a modified form. Sometimes the New Testament writers, and even our Lord, have been charged with “inaccuracies.”

These verbal changes have been explained by some, on the theory that the inspiration of the Bible extends not to the “words, but to the concept,” or thought; or that New Testament writers take liberties with scripture and modify their quotations as modern authors might, in citing passages from Shakespeare or Milton. Such 'explanations' are too loose and only increase our embarrassment. We venture to suggest a more reverent method of accounting for such changes, viz.: that, where New Testament authors, in quoting, adopt the Septuagint version or change the exact language of the original Hebrew, the Spirit guided them so to do, in order to bring more clearly to view the inspired meaning of sacred words.

Oftentimes a reason may be discovered for such modification. In Heb. xi. 40, 1 Pet. i. 11,12, etc., we are taught that Old Testament writers themselves wrote much that they did not themselves understand, and that was left on record for after ages to interpret. May it not be that, when New Testament writers are led by the Spirit of God to quote these words, they are also led in some cases to modify them so as to throw upon the original quotation the new light of a more perfect day? Compare Ps. xl. 7-8, with Heb. x. 5-10. Only after our Lord became incarnate, could it be understood *how* He came to do God's will "in a body prepared."

Compare Isa. lxi. 1,2, with Luke iv. 18, 19. Mal. iii. 1, with Mark i. 2, "before Thy face."

2. There is likewise a progressive revelation of *morality*.

The ethical standard of the gospel age is far in advance of the Levitical: and the rule of conduct must be graduated and estimated by the fuller, clearer revelation of duty and of love.

"To him that knoweth to do good and doeth it not, to him it is sin." Jas. iv. 17. "If ye know these things, happy are ye if ye do them." Jno. xiii. 17.

"The times of this ignorance God winked at." Acts xvii. 30.

Such texts as these teach us that:

> The object of knowledge is practice; and
> The scope of practice is knowledge.

The rule of duty is relative: "To whom much is given, of him will much be required;" more light demands better life.

Patriarchs, in practising polygamy, deception, human servitude; in inflicting penalty without legal process, etc., are not to be judged by the New Testament principles not in their day clearly revealed. Things but dimly seen if at all at dawn, are clearly and boldly revealed at noon-day.

3. There is particularly a Progressive Revelation as to *missions*, or the duty of believers to the unsaved about them.

It is true that the Bible is throughout a missionary book. Missions are taught in the Old Testament, but it is as in a mirror, darkly, dimly, enigmatically, as truth is taught in parables. Practically the old time saints did not conceive of God's people as having an aggressive mission to "make disciples of all nations," nor did they conceive of other nations as subjects of converting grace. To them, the heathen were simply obstacles to the prosperity, progress and even existence, of the one God-fearing, elect people; and even Peter the apostle had to learn, by a thrice repeated vision on the housetop, that the old exclusiveness must be broken down before the inclusiveness of the Christian spirit.

Much of the so called 'vindictive spirit' of the "Imprecatory" psalms and prophetic utterances should be interpreted as the breathing of a holy jealousy for God, and a devout desire to have all foes of the true faith destroyed, or at least dispersed. Compare Ps. lix. 11.

General Suggestions – Laws of Interpretation, Etc.

We now add some general remarks, intended to be suggestive especially as to the principles upon which biblical studies should be pursued; and we lay down certain obvious laws of interpretation and canons of criticism.

I. The Bible is imperial in source, divine in authority, original in contents, and infallible in teaching. But it abounds in *mysterious truths,* and is often *paradoxical in statement.*

Both the mystery and the paradox are necessary features of the Word of God, as the Book itself concedes. But it does not follow that what we cannot solve is insoluble or absurd. Deut. xxix. 29, 1 Cor. ii. 11.

II. Apparent discrepancies are inseparable from the Word of God.

The natural universe abounds in inscrutable mysteries and seeming contradictions. Nature is the arena of perpetual conflict. With all the undeniable evidences of design, there are occasional monstrosities; and, side by side with proofs of benevolence in the Creator, there are gigantic forms of disaster and destruction.

So in the Bible. The Trinity and Unity of Godhead; the Sovereignty of God and the freedom of man; the Divine Immutability and the promises to praying souls; — paradoxes like these inhere in the nature of God and of divine truth, and in the limited faculty and knowledge of man.

That God ever began to be is impossible and inconceivable; yet that God had no beginning is equally an inscrutable mystery, for how did He ever reach the present stage of His existence! If an Eternity is already passed, why may not an Eternal future reach its end? Whoever attempts to think on such themes will soon learn that there are limits to human reason. The idea of succession must not enter into our conception of Eternity; yet, of duration without succession we cannot now conceive.

III. We must settle the limits of Inspiration.

Much of the Word of God consists of simply an inspired narrative, in which all that Inspiration covers or guarantees is the *accuracy* and *veracity* of the record. This principle seems to us so obvious, that, like an axiom, it needs only a statement. One may give a most exact and truthful account of what has taken place, while disapproving the whole transaction which is recorded. We must therefore in every case notice the *authorship* and *authority* of all statements or sentiments found in the sacred book.

"*Verbal Inspiration*" is to some persons a very obnoxious term, but when it is properly understood we see no ground of objection to it. It means only this, as we use it: that the Inspiring Spirit guided, guarded and governed *the very language in which God's thought was expressed by holy men*, who not only *thought*, but "*spake* as they were moved by the Holy Ghost." Who is there that holds every word of the Bible to be in the same sense, inspired? When Satan says, "Ye shall not surely die;" when Job and his three friends discuss the problem and philosophy of evil; when the blind man, whose eyes were opened by Christ, argues with the Pharisees; when, in a word, the Bible narrates human events or records human utterances in which God is not represented either as acting or speaking through man, inspiration covers only the essential *accuracy of the narrative*. But when God directs a course to be pursued, or himself guides an utterance, the sanction of His infallible authority is thus given. We are not unduly jealous that "degrees of inspiration" be disallowed, provided that the lowest degree of inspiration shall guard infallibility. For without this the Bible becomes simply the best of books; and loses all its divine character as the final court of appeal — the Judge which, when wit and wisdom fail, ends the strife. Men crave, and will have, a final arbiter.

We are more and more impressed with the exactness and accuracy of Scripture. When, for instance, Matthew records the direct fulfillment of a specific prediction he says: "that it might be fulfilled which was spoken by *the prophet*;"' but when he refers to Christ's hailing from Nazareth, he says: "that it might be fulfilled which was spoken by the *prophets*,"' (plural) "He shall be called a Nazarene" — for not in the writings of any *one* prophet, but rather in the drift of all prophecy is this forecast found. And so, on the day of Pentecost, Peter does not say, "then was *fulfilled* that which was spoken by the prophet Joel; but, "*this is that which was spoken*" — for, although the outpouring of Pentecost finds its only *explanation* in Joel, the *fulfilment* of that prophecy is yet to come, when the Spirit, then poured out on all *disciples*, shall be "poured out upon all *flesh*."

Two Greek words are translated "speech," "discourse" or "saying," (λογος ρημα) yet only *one* (λογος) is ever applied to Christ. If God did not guide the *words* used, why were such distinctions so carefully preserved? And this is but one case out of hundreds familiar to any Bible student. There are "concepts" of God which no existing Greek words could express, and a new nomenclature had to be created, or new meanings attached to formerly existing words. The New Testament must have a glossary of its own; for a classical dictionary would not suffice. The more deeply we immerse ourselves in the study of the original Scriptures, the more will the divine choice of words impress us.

There are certainly five passages of Scripture which may be cited as giving no uncertain sound on the subject of "Verbal Inspiration" (Compare Heb. xii. 27, John x. 34-36, Gal. iii. 16, Gal. iv. 9, and John viii. 58.) In the first, the argument turns on the significance of a single *phrase*; in the second, on the inviolability of a single *word*; in the third, on the use of a singular, instead of a plural *number*; in the fourth, on the passive, instead of the active, *voice* of a verb; and in the fifth, on the use of the present, instead of the past, *tense* of the verb. Taking the five together, we are taught that “the Scripture must not be broken,” so far as to change a *phrase*, a *word*, the *number* of a noun, or the *voice* or *tense* of a verb. If that is not verbal inspiration — a divine oversight extending not only to “concept,” but to language — our “'scholarship” is entirely at fault, and we are glad that it is!

Of course, no inspiration can be claimed, in any such sense, for the various *translations or versions* of the original Scriptures. Human language is but a mirror or camera, before which we place the Word of God, to catch its reflection or image. The reflection or image will be imperfect, just so far as the mirror, or the camera, with its lenses and sensitive plates, is imperfect; yet for all practical purposes, these translations and versions are as faithful and accurate reproductions as the reflected image and the photographic likeness, which are but the “counterfeit presentments” of the man, and not the man himself; and such translations do not seriously mislead any candid reader.

IV. The Inspiration of Scripture must certainly secure *inerrancy* and *infallibility*; otherwise every man is at liberty to determine for himself what he accepts or rejects.

Some who deny the inerrancy of Scripture, concede that these "errors are all in the circumstantials, and not in the essentials." But who shall decide what are "essentials" and what "circumstantials?" As a huge door turns upon a very small hinge, stupendous events hang upon what is seemingly insignificant. In God's universe there are no little things. If we admit errors in the original Scriptures, any modern Jehudi may, with his penknife, cut out from the sacred scroll whatever he pleases; and on the "authority" of his reason, and perhaps, of his "church," decide that the exscinded part belongs not to " essentials" but to "'circumstantials."

Current popular phraseology which is known to be scientifically inaccurate, may find its way into the Bible simply as a prevailing *idiom of speech*. It is common to speak of the "Battle of Bunker Hill," though every reader of our history knows that Breed's Hill was the actual scene of the battle. The phrases "rising and setting sun," "dew descending" from heaven, etc., though found in the Word of God, argue no essential error, because these current forms of speech, — the "language of appearances" — are universal even where known to be scientifically inaccurate.

Each apparent error in the Word of God must be accounted for by itself. Many errors may be traced to sources already indicated, and possibly some we may not now be able to trace. But to admit the principle that the "scriptures abound in errors, inaccuracies, mistakes and immoralities" is to destroy the value of the Bible as the Word of God.

V. We must come to the study of the Word of God with *clear and discriminating minds.*

1. Our tests must be sensible, rational tests.

In Heb. vi. 18, we are told that it is "impossible for God to lie." But again we are told in Matt. xix. 26, that "with God all things are possible." There is no contradiction. It is only the silly caviller who cries out, "God cannot be omnipotent, because He cannot lie." This is no limitation of God's power; for power can be tested only within the proper sphere and range of power. The impossibility of God's lying is not a physical but a moral impossibility, and if the same impossibility existed in some cavillers, such a dishonest objection and disingenuous argument would never have been brought forward.

2. We must use sanctified common sense.

God knows all men, omnisciently; yet He says of Abraham, "'Now, I know that thou fearest God," etc., as though it were a new discovery. Gen. xxii. 12. Here He means that He had *verified*, by experiment, Abraham's faithfulness; it was an *eventual* knowing. So when God is said to have "remembered Noah" (Gen. viii. 1), it is not implied that He had ever forgotten him ; but there is indicated and recorded an *active* remembrance, evinced in what He did to bring Noah again out of the ark in safety.

3. In studying the Divine anger against sin, we must beware of attributing to God a *merciless severity*, because He judicially destroys the ungodly.

Mercy to others sometimes makes severity to offenders the only course compatible with either justice or love to the universe at large. Chief Justice Hale said, "When I am tempted to be merciful to offenders, let me remember that there is also a mercy due to my country." Prince Eugene never pardoned certain offenders, whom the Duke of Marlborough generally dealt with leniently. But it was found on comparison of records that, with all his laxity, the duke had been compelled to hang many more such offenders than the prince, because the duke's laxity encouraged such to hope for immunity from penalty. We must beware of *unregenerate notions of benevolence.*

4. We must learn to distinguish between what is *literal* and what is *spiritual.*

Many difficulties arise from confusion here: on the one hand we may literalize what is to be spiritually interpreted, or we may spiritualize what is to be literally understood.

For example, “Israel,” “Zion,” and “the church” are often used by us as though they were equivalent expressions. Paul draws in 1 Cor. x. 32, a distinction which, if always borne in mind, will greatly assist in Bible study: “The Jews, the Gentiles, and the Church of God” are the three factors, never to be confounded in the study of the Word.

When we are told to “call no man your father upon earth” (Matt. xxiii. 9), to understand this literally would be to forbid any child to address his father as such! When we are told, “swear not at all” (Matt. v. 34), literally construed, this would forbid an "oath for confirmation" in a court of justice. Paul writes (1 Tim. vi. 16), that God “only hath immortality;” does he mean that the human soul, the angels, and even the Lord Jesus, are not immortal? When, in Rom. xvi. 27, we read of “God only wise,” are we to infer that there is no such thing as a wise man?

Annihilationists argue from the phrase in Ps. xxxvii. 9, 34, that “evil doers shall be *cut off*” (karath), that they are utterly to *perish*. But this same word is used of Messiah — Dan. ix. 26.

Cardinal Bellarmine argued from two texts, John xxi. 16, “feed my sheep,” and Acts x. 13, “'rise — kill and eat,” that the successors of Peter, the Roman Pontiffs, have a double duty — to *feed true believers and to kill heretics*. Why did he not go to the full length of his literalism, and insist that the popes should "eat" the heretics they "'kill?" (See Haley, 280).

VI. We must discriminate between a *part* and *the whole*. A part neither includes nor excludes all the rest which belongs to the complete form.

Take for example the *Inscription on the Cross*. The full form was this:

"THIS IS JESUS OF NAZARETH,
THE KING OF THE JEWS."

Of these ten words, Mark records five, Luke seven, Matthew and John, each, eight; but no two evangelists give either the whole inscription, or select the same words from the whole. To assume that any one intends to give the whole inscription will of course make harmony impossible; but to assume that each gives so much, and such a part, of the whole as suits the *precise object* of his narrative, relieves the various accounts from all antagonism or inaccuracy.

VII. *Exceptions do not invalidate a rule*, they rather prove it. This is a common canon of all criticism, and has numerous applications to the contents of Scripture.

VIII. *Hypotheses may be of great value*, in unlocking mysteries and obscurities, and settling doubts.

It has long been an established law of all scientific inquiry, that, wherever a supposition meets all the facts of a given case and removes all objections, it may be safely adopted as the solution. Kepler sought to find the true theory of the universe, and applied *eighteen* successive hypotheses before be discovered the Harmonic Laws. His final hypothesis answered all conditions, like a perfectly fitting key in a lock, and it was admitted as the true solution of planetary orbits, etc. Upon the basis of a mere *supposition* the old Ptolemaic theory of the universe was finally overturned and the true nature of planetary motion discovered.

In the study of Scripture truth, let us not be driven from a *satisfactory hypothesis* which serves as an explanation, because our adversaries clamor for “positive” or "mathematical" proofs. The burden lies with them, to prove the hypothesis untenable and the solution unsatisfactory.

IX. The *fact*, the *nature* and *the uses of Paradox* in Scripture, should be carefully noted.

A Paradox is an apparent contradiction where real harmony exists; a seeming absurdity which is still a fact, or a truth. The famous “Hydrostatic” and “mechanical” paradoxes will illustrate this principle.

There are in Scripture *three sorts* of paradoxes.

1. The *Proverbial.* Proverbs xxvi. 4, 5.

> “Answer a fool, according to his folly;”
> “Answer not a fool according to his folly.”

The reconciliation is plain: there are cases in which a course, proper at other times, is unwise. A fool may ask a question, to answer which may be to identify one's self with his folly: again he may ask a question, to answer which may be to show him his folly.

2. The *Doctrinal.*

Philippians ii. 12, *Work out* your own salvation, for it is God which *worketh in* you both to will and to do.

No man *can come* to me except the Father draw him:

Ye *will not come* to me, etc. John vi. 44; v. 40.

3. The *Prophetical.*

Isaiah liii. abounds in these — there are in this chapter at least *twelve*:

Christ was a Root out of dry ground, yet fruitful; Christ was without form or beauty, yet God's elect Servant; Christ was despised and rejected, yet the accepted Messiah; Christ was the Suffering and Dying, yet Living Saviour; Christ was without generation, yet having numerous Seed; Christ was making grave with the wicked, yet with the rich; Christ was in adversity, yet in prosperity; Christ was defeated and despoiled, yet conquering and despoiling; Christ was cut off in the midst of days, yet prolonging his days; Christ was condemned himself, yet satisfying many, etc., etc.

The Uses of Discrepancies

We now approach one final question;

Do these so called *Discrepancies* serve any Providential purpose?

We cannot believe that they are wholly accidental; and a careful and reflective study will show us that they do answer certain very important ends. A few of these it may be well to mention.

I. These apparent discrepancies serve first of all to show us that the Author of the Bible has *guarded even its text from essential corruptions.*

How little all these discrepancies amount to in the aggregate, is amazing. With all these extant manuscripts and all the various sources whence they emanate, the text of the scriptures is in all vital matters essentially unimpaired.

The variations are numerous but unimportant. They consist of differences in orthography, in the selection and collocation of words, and other minor matters. In the Hebrew manuscripts over three quarters of a million of various readings may be counted, as to *consonants* alone, and so we may say, in proportion, of the New Testament. But they are of little or no account in the main, and do not affect the sense any more than the different spellings of such words as 'fulfil,' 'plough,' etc.

The Masorites, superstitiously punctilious as they were, became, in the Providence of God, guardians of the text of sacred scripture. They counted, classified and recorded, verses, words, and even letters, so that the Bible has come down to us with a text purer and more certain than that of any other ancient book. In the manuscripts of Terence, and within a much less space than our New Testament, Dr. Bentley found 20,000 various lections, and affirmed his belief that upon further search he would more than double the number of such discoveries.

In the manuscripts, collated for Griesbach's Testament, 150,000 various readings occur. Yet it is remarkable that, notwithstanding these hundreds of thousands of variations, the substance of scripture is not, by any of them, or by all of them together, *materially affected*; not one article of faith, not one moral duty, not one theological doctrine, not one essential truth, is in the slightest modified. The variations are mostly trivial, relating mainly to the names, numbers, dates, or to the letters of words. And the grand result is that, with the exception of perhaps from a dozen to twenty verses, the text of every chapter, paragraph and even sentence of scripture, is now so firmly settled that only the *meaning* is open to doubt or dispute.

Compare this result with the results of the study of Shakespearian manuscripts. (See Haley, 47.)

II. These discrepancies serve to *awaken and stimulate intellectual inquiry* and *investigation*. It is the study which these apparent disagreements have made necessary, by which we have been led to the discovery of the purest text.

As variations were found, they naturally compelled a searching and scholarly comparison of all extant manuscripts. To ascertain the exact date and source of each manuscript, to investigate into the period of its origin and the claims which it possessed to recognition, caused a vast expenditure of learning, time and pains. And the consequence is that, as families have traced their lineage for ages, into a remote past, so we have developed a new and distinct science, that may be called the "*Genealogy of the Manuscripts*" Compare Westcott and Hort's Introduction to the New Testament.

III. These discrepancies furthermore teach us that, valuable as is the *letter* of scripture, *the truth* which it conveys is of vastly higher importance.

God permitted slight variations to find their way into the text, while He preserved the testimony of all the manuscripts essentially uniform, unvarying and consistent; and thus we are led to look supremely, not at the divergence, but at the convergence of their testimony in one burning focal point of harmonious truth.

IV. These discrepancies have *established the Independence and Integrity of the sacred writers.*

There may be *too close* a correspondence in the testimony of witnesses; what was intended to confirm may thus tend to condemn. The entire absence of seeming collision, even in trifling details or minutiae, argues intentional collusion, or conspiracy to deceive.

In courts of law, evidence, given by different parties, which exactly and minutely agrees, is presumptive proof of a previous arrangement. For instance, in New Bedford, the famous "Howland will" case involved $2,000,000, and $150,000 were spent in costs of a trial extending over two years. The whole issue turned upon the resemblance between two signatures both of which were claimed as Miss

Rowland's. So precisely, however, did the second match the first, that it was held to be a forged imitation.

Those who cavil at slight variations in the gospel narratives, forget that the test of truthful testimony on the part of witnesses, is *substantial agreement with circumstantial variations.*

V. These discrepancies have rather *proven the real value of the Word of God.*

For more than fifteen centuries the complete Bible has been the target of malignant, bitter hostility and assault. Every expedient of learning as well as ridicule has been exhausted to overthrow it. It has been subjected to microscopic scrutiny, and yet these insignificant 'defects,' as they are assumed to be by the enemies of the truth and by some so called friends, are all that can be found to justify the opposition to the Bible as the inspired, inerrant, infallible Word of God !

Rev. J. H. Brookes, D. D., of St. Louis, once offered $500.00 reward to anyone who would point out a single irreconcilable contradiction in the Word of God. After four weeks' study a sceptic claimed the reward: he had made the great discovery, and here it is:

"Matthew xii. 30. He that is not with me is against me."
"Luke ix. 50. He that is not against us is for us (!!)."

VI. These discrepancies are used of God to *instruct the docile believer.*

Christ told his disciples that he used *Parables* so that truth might at once be veiled from the unteachable and yet revealed to the obedient and docile. For the same reason God uses contradictions. *Paradoxes are parables*; by the very contrariety which they exhibit they stimulate thought, and arouse curiosity; by the effort to reconcile them we are sometimes more profited than by any mere comparison of similar statements. Compare John xv. 15, and xvi. 12.

Prophetic paradoxes serve also another use: they are designed as Enigmas, presenting a mystery to be afterwards solved by the event. Thus the mystery which they suggest becomes a lock, to which history becomes the *key*; and the perfect fitting of key and lock proves a divine hand in both the prophecy and the history. Compare Ezek. xii. 13, with Jer. xxxix. 7.

Proverbial paradoxes compel reflection by their apparent divergence, just as views in a stereoscope often make necessary a fixed and patient gaze, in order to bring the two pictures into harmony and unity. We find after careful study that the two members of a paradox are evidently meant to balance each other, each helping to limit, extend, qualify or modify its complementary member. They present extremes between which we are to find the golden mean of truth, as the mariner finds it his safe course to steer midway between two headlands, or as the mechanician produces a resultant by using two forces which act at right angles to each other. (See Haley.)

VII. These discrepancies also become a test of the *candor and genuineness of the Bible reader or student.*

The great Teacher presented truth in forms suited to attract the truth lover, but to repel the hypocritical and insincere. His teaching thus became a *sifting* process, separating the real from the nominal followers. See John vi. 35-69. In this case those who heard Christ's words "murmured at him," "strove among themselves," called them "hard sayings," were "offended," and some "went back and walked no more with him." Yet it will be seen that, with every increase of their opposition, Christ, instead of modifying and mollifying his teaching, rather increased its apparent severity. He knew that each concession to unbelief and an unteachable spirit, would only embolden the demand for new concessions. When the disobedient stumbled at his saying, instead of retracting or qualifying his statement, he at least repeated it, in even in its obnoxious form. Compare John iii. 3-7.

Our Lord seemed to give, to such as sought it, an occasion of stumbling. When modern teachers find any statement of truth, such as the sovereignty of God, an occasion of offence to a hearer, they make haste to soften and qualify it. Just now the church universal is busy revising creeds, as though to adapt them to the demands of a worldly type of Christian character, and a rationalistic spirit. Let us remember that by every concession we make reason bolder in its demand that everything shall be squared to its measure. Christ in pursuing just the contrary course taught his hearers to bow implicitly and submit with docility to the truth — or else he left them to stumble over it and fall and be broken.

VIII. Thus these discrepancies also *discipline the true believer to yield an unquestioning obedience to the truth.*

Reason has its province: (a) to determine upon rational grounds of evidence whether or not the Bible be the word of God; (b) then to determine what that word teaches; and (c) what are the relations or bearings of its teaching upon one's self and one's duty. Beyond this the province of reason ceases, and the province of faith and obedience begins. For instance prophecy is of great significance and consequence, as it is *one,* if not the *main one,* of those "seven seals" set by God as His sanction upon His Word. Other evidences may appeal to *believers* as more satisfactory, but these evidences demand faith for their recognition, reception and appreciation. When an *inquirer* comes, in doubt and darkness, to the Bible, to find proofs that it *is the Word of God,* and therefore has a claim on his faith, predictive prophecy is God's grand appeal to his reason. "We have also a more sure word of prophecy, whereunto ye do well that ye take heed as unto a light that shineth in a dark place, *until the day dawn* and the day star arise in your hearts."

In fact our perception of truth largely depends upon our *spiritual attainment.* Hence paradoxes are often reconciled by simple obedience. Jno. vii. 17. By doing His will we come to know the doctrine. There is a hidden harmony — a higher harmony that is hidden from us — until we yield up our whole soul and self to God for service, and yield up our whole heart and mind to truth in reverence.

Many so called discrepancies are due to the disposition and determination of unfair and uncandid critics; "*aut inveniam discrepentiam aut faciam*" What Whately says about wise men and fools may be said about objectors: It is easier to ask, than to answer, a question, and many a man can present a difficulty who could not remove it.

In Voltaire's library a Swedish traveler found Calmet's Commentary, with slips of paper inserted, on which all the difficulties Calmet had treated were carefully noted, but *not one of the answers and solutions* whereby he met and refuted them.

Prof. Henry Rogers says, that Strauss' "Life of Jesus" should be called, "a collection of all the difficulties and discrepancies which honest criticism has discovered, or perverted ingenuity imagined, in the four evangelists." (Haley 27, 28.)

Thus what veils truth from carnal minds may reveal it to the spiritual: and the same doctrine that is a *stumbling stone* to the unbeliever is a *stepping stone* to the believer, i Pet. ii. 8.

IX. The obscurity of scripture is probably made to serve *to godless reader's a judicial end.*

The captious, cavilling critic is punished by *finding* the very snares which he seeks, and falling into them. Perhaps he tries to make faith impossible in others, and ends by making his own mind simply a nest of objections, a perch for the unclean birds of doubt and denial of truth, so that faith can find no resting place in himself. He tries in a dishonest spirit to prove the Word of God a human fraud and falsehood, and is himself given over by God to believe what at the beginning he knew was a lie. He, who did not like to retain God in his knowledge, and who held down the truth in unrighteousness, and sought to turn the truth of God into a lie, is given over to a reprobate mind. The Judge of all abandons him to strong delusion.

X. Where all attempts at explanation or reconciliation fail, the believer must learn *patiently to wait for the further light which dissolves all doubt*.

This introduces another department of the subject, which the author has extensively treated in another work entitled "Many Infallible Proofs."

The investigation into discrepancies has served to reveal hundreds and thousands of agreements which would not otherwise have been disclosed, and which are truly wonderful as the evidences of the divine authorship of the Bible, as well as of the integrity of the human agents which the Spirit of God employed in its production.

The Bible has been decried and derided as in hopeless opposition to science and irreconcilable conflict with modern discovery. But the further the investigation is carried the more marvelous proves the agreement between the word of God and the most advanced certainties attained by science.

The substantial agreement between the story of the creation and the discoveries of geology; the word "firmament" or *expanse*, as applied to the space between the heavens and the earth; the order of creation, from the lowest types to the highest — fish, reptile, bird, mammal, man; the countless number of the stars (Jer. xxxiii. 22) , the four supports of life – brain, lungs, heart, nervous system, with the circulation of the blood (Eccles. xii. 6, 7); the nature of light, as called forth, not "made" (Gen. i,); and as a mode of motion or vibration akin to sound or music (Job xxxviii. 7, Ps. lxv. 8, — *Hebrew*, to give forth vibrations — Ps. xix. etc.); these are a very few of the startling agreements between the Bible and scientific facts *not known by man* until long after the Bible was complete!

Modern believing scientists may well ask, how the infidel can account for such anticipations of modern discovery. Compare Ps. cxix. 32, with the fact that the staghound, fleetest in chase, has the largest heart, in comparison to his size, of any animal. The ant's brain is entirely composed of the *gray* matter, whose preponderance in the brain is the measure of intelligence. Compare Prov. vi. 6. The *agricultural* ant does prepare a harvest — as recent investigation shows — and Solomon did not blunder in taking for *grain* the ant eggs or pupae. Compare Prov. xxx. 25. Man *was* made of the dust of the ground — and the most recent analysis shows his identity in material substance with the ground on which he treads, etc., etc. Compare Gen. i. and ii.

To those who wish to examine the wonderful agreement of the Bible with the facts of *history* — one of the foremost of sciences — we commend the careful study of *prophecy*, even to its *minute details*, for the *minute* details of prophecy are vital to the prophetic proofs; it is these minutiae that remove a prediction from the realm of sagacious human forecast into that of divinely inspired foresight. It is these also that make the difference between the law of "simple" and of "compound probability." Every single prediction has but a *half chance* of fulfillment; and hence every additional detail *halves again* the possibility of a mere accidental accomplishment. In the Old Testament the *predictions* concerning Messiah, which are most indisputable as predictions, because most undeniably remote from the events which they foretell, are also the most astonishingly minute in their details. The late Canon Liddon, in his famous Bampton lectures, gives three hundred and thirty-three particulars, prophesied about Messiah, and all meeting in him alone. By the law of compound probability we must raise one-half to its three hundred and thirty-second power to get the insignificant fraction which represents the possibility of a chance fulfillment; that fraction will have, as its numerator, a unit, and its denominator will reach *ninety-four places*! Who audaciously dares to say that the slightest particular is of no consequence? The ancestral line, the exact place, time, and circumstances of Christ's birth, with hundreds of most curiously minute marks, go to make up and complete that Old Testament portraiture of the "Coming One;" and, even when Christ hung upon the cross, he could not say, "It is finished!" and expire, until the last and least Scripture should "be fulfilled;" and so He said, "I thirst!" And yet that forecast of his dying agony was not in a formal prediction, but in a Psalm, a poem whose true meaning is read only when in its jewelled cavern the Light of the World is set!

In a portrait, the entire fidelity of the resemblance may depend upon *one line* which changes or determines that subtle thing called "expression!" One delicate touch on the eyebrow, the turn or curve of an almost invisible line about the mouth, a tinge or a shade of color on the cheek, a vein in the forehead, one dainty stroke in that concave of the upper lip — these make the difference between the work of the master artist and his amateur pupils. And the Holy Ghost proves himself the Divine Artist, more if possible by his most minute and delicate strokes and touches than by his bolder and more conspicuous outlines. What was, at first, a drawing without color, at last becomes a complete, recognizable portrait.

CONCLUSION.

The grand purpose and aim we have had in view in this little book, has been to exalt the *supremacy of scripture*. Various attempts are making, in these days, to impair confidence in the claim of the Bible to be the Inspired and Infallible Word of God, and the supreme guide in faith and duty. We are in the midst of the war of the ages, and the enemy is assaulting the center and stronghold of the Christian religion; for with its Sacred *Book* is inseparably bound up its Sacred *Person*.

Some of the friends of the Bible seek to accommodate themselves to the positions of its foes, by giving up the infallibility and inerrancy of the scripture, and conceding that there are "mistakes" and even "immoralities" in the Bible; but such defenders of the Word of God claim that its inspiration is to be found not in the "words" but the "concept."

We regard this position as wholly untenable, and as a virtual surrender of the Bible as a Divine Book. And we lift up a warning against such views, by whomsoever promulgated.

The contents of this Book of Books are especially made emphatic in its very title, "The Word of God." Repeatedly does the expression occur, "*Words* which I command thee," etc. Paul echoes the Old Testament sentiment in the New: "which things also we speak, *not in words which man's wisdom teacheth, but which the Holy Ghost teacheth*."' And he adds, "comparing spiritual things with spiritual," which, by not a few, is regarded as a simple expansion of the meaning i. e., "expressing spiritual truths in spiritual forms."

Wordsworth says, "Language is the incarnation of thought." Burke regarded every word in a sentence as one of the feet on which the sentence walks; and said that, to alter a word, change it for a longer or shorter one, or give it a different position, might change the whole course of the sentence.

There are in the Bible thousands of cases in which the accuracy of the "concept" depends on the exactness of the "word," and even of the shade of meaning which it conveys and by which it is separated from others of its class. When God sought to convey to man an adequate "concept" of spiritual truth, the task was the more difficult from the fact that heavenly things were to be conveyed to earthly minds and through earthly channels. How could even God impart a knowledge of such matters without leaving the door open to serious, if not fatal, error, unless he guided, at least by supervision and control, the very words in which divine conceptions were clothed?

No reader of the New Testament Greek needs to be told that the whole Epistle to the Romans turns on a single word (δικαιοσυνη); and so important is it that the reader shall not misunderstand that word, and the *exact sense* in which it is employed, that in Rom. iii. 25-26, the meaning is exactly and repeatedly defined, "To declare, I say, at this time *his righteousness*: that He might be just and the justifier of him that believeth in Jesus." That is righteousness, in the sense of this epistle. Are we to be told that the concept is the inspired thing, not the word? How are we to get the true concept apart from the right word? To form a wrong conception of justification, as here used, is to misconceive that doctrinal truth which lies at the very basis of our salvation. There are over five thousand instances in Old and New Testaments where the most important distinctions hang on the choice of a particular word, and no other, however like it, will suffice.

It is unsafe to make the Bible and the Church, and the human Reason joint, or co-ordinate, sources of divine authority. Both the Church and Reason are authoritative only as they are conformed to, and are confirmed by, the Word of God. The voice of our rational powers, and even the *communis consensus Christianorum*, like the fallible standards of weights and measures, need correction by the infallible, as the watch is regulated by the chronometer, and even the chronometer by God's clock, the stars. The mariner dares not follow even his compass as an absolute guide, lest he lose his course, if not his vessel. The needle may have intensity of directive force and susceptibility, but it has its variations; the magnetic pole must be corrected by the celestial pole. Reason and conscience, and even the verdict of the Church, all belong to the human and fallible, and we must steer by the constellations.

The *supremacy of the Word of God* is the last great truth which is the Palladium of Church and the believer. When that falls, all else falls with it No disaster is too great to follow the destruction of that safeguard of Protestantism. And we should look well before we admit any teaching which actually surrenders this inmost citadel of our faith, or even by implication weakens or lessens the absolute supremacy of the word of God.

We therefore earnestly ask all who wish to know the truth and find the hidden treasures of the Word, not to be kept from a thorough exploration of its hidden beauties by any apparent and superficial discordancies and disagreements. These are but the iron gates that seem forbidding but that yield to the touch of a reverent and obedient spirit and admit us to the "House Beautiful."

And a Beautiful Palace it is, "built upon the *foundation* of the apostles and Prophets, Jesus Christ himself being the chief corner-stone." In *formation*, composed of the most precious materials faintly typified in the cedar and shittim woods, and the gold, silver and precious stones. In *construction*, it follows the law of a divine unity and archetypal beauty. In *completeness*, it is divinely perfect. The believer finds all his wants and cravings met. In its refectory it has milk for babes, and the manna, the meat, the honey, for strong men; in its lavatory are the fountains of the water and the blood, that cleanse and sanctify; in its pharmacy, the balm of Gilead and the panacea for all ills of sin; in its armory, the whole panoply of God; in its gallery, the portraits of the prophets, patriarchs, apostles and saints; in its oratory, the altars of sacrifice and incense, prayer and praise; in its conservatory, the celestial plants that bloom in the paradise of God; and in its observatory, the outlook into the very heavens, where we may behold the face of God.

Blessed is he who enters into all the wonders of God's “House Beautiful” whose vestibule is so low and whose doors are so narrow that only the humble and obedient soul, who bows as he goes in, can enter at all; and whose inmost wonders are to be seen only in the clear light of the Holy Spirit's guidance, who with celestial lamps illumines the secrets of God to him who, in dependence on the great Interpreter, searches the scriptures.

With the prayer that each reader may learn to find in what, to the profane and godless, are a stone of stumbling and a rock of offence, the stepping stones to higher knowledge and faith, the author bids his reader

FAREWELL!

You may obtain this and many other fine resources published by Fountain of Life Ministries by contacting us:

Web:
www.hbcfrankfort.org

Email:
heritagebaptistchurch@att.net

Postal Mail:
Fountain of Life Ministries
202 Brynn Drive
Manhattan, IL 60442
United States of America

www.ingramcontent.com/pod-product-compliance
Ingram Content Group UK Ltd.
Pitfield, Milton Keynes, MK11 3LW, UK
UKHW041840200726
13854UKWH00003BA/1235

9 781105 555589